GEOMETRIC QUILTS

Created for Leisure Arts by House of White Birches

GEOMETRIC QUILTS

LEISURE ARTS STAFF
Editor-in-Chief **Susan White Sullivan**
Quilt Publications Director **Cheryl Johnson**
Special Projects Director **Susan Frantz Wiles**
Senior Prepress Director **Mark Hawkins**
Art Publications Director **Rhonda Shelby**
Imaging Technician **Stephanie Johnson**
Prepress Technician **Janie Marie Wright**
Publishing Systems Administrator **Becky Riddle**
Mac Information Technology Specialist **Robert Young**

President and Chief Executive Officer **Rick Barton**
Vice President of Sales **Mike Behar**
Director of Finance and Administration **Laticia Mull Dittrich**
National Sales Director **Martha Adams**
Creative Services **Chaska Lucas**
Information Technology Director **Hermine Linz**
Controller **Francis Caple**
Vice President, Operations **Jim Dittrich**
Retail Customer Service Manager **Stan Raynor**
Print Production Manager **Fred F. Pruss**

HOUSE OF WHITE BIRCHES STAFF
Editor **Jeanne Stauffer**
Art Director **Brad Snow**
Publishing Services Director **Brenda Gallmeyer**
Editorial Assistant **Stephanie Franklin**
Assistant Art Director **Nick Pierce**
Copy Supervisor **Deborah Morgan**
Copy Editors **Emily Carter, Mary O'Donnell**
Technical Proofreader **Angie Buckles**
Production Artist Supervisor **Erin Augsburger**
Graphic Artist **Jessi Butler**
Production Assistants **Marj Morgan, Judy Neuenschwander**
Technical Artist **Debera Kuntz**
Photography Supervisor **Tammy Christian**
Photography **Scott Campbell, Matthew Owen**
Photo Stylists **Tammy Liechty, Tammy Steiner**

Library of Congress Control Number: 2011927789

ISBN-13/EAN: 978-1-60900-357-9

10 9 8 7 6 5 4 3 2 1

Introduction

Discover the fun of using color, block placement and shape to add an extra dimension to your quilting.

Although all quilts are geometric in the strictest sense of the word since they are designs based on simple geometric shapes (as straight lines, circles or squares), some projects have an added element that sets them apart.

In some cases, the shape of the project itself is not the usual rectangle. The first project in the book has paper-pieced triangles and squares, but places them in such an arrangement that the table runner has a very unique shape. Another project with an unusual shape is the wall quilt titled Window to the World, which uses bright-color blades appliquéd to a black background. The wall quilt Sound Waves places triangles in such an arrangement that they look like they are vibrating.

Other projects use a combination of blocks to create unusual shapes within the quilt. Arabesque counterpoints a typical block made of squares and triangles with a neighboring block that has a variation of the Drunkard's Path design at each corner. Add in an unusual placement of fabrics, and a distinctive secondary design is created for this wall quilt. The bed quilt Well-Connected Stars also uses the placement of two blocks side by side and the use of color to create an eye-catching secondary design.

Other designs use light and dark fabrics to emphasize the geometric shape within a quilt. The table runner Chained Lightning uses brightly colored, scrappy triangles on a white background to create a secondary diamond design. Casablanca is an excellent quilt for studying the secondary designs that can be made with the placement of lights and darks. The quilt is pieced from triangles and squares, but you can see several secondary shapes in the completed wall quilt.

Take your quilting to the next level by using color, block placement and different shapes to create interesting quilt projects. It's easy and fun to do.

TABLE OF CONTENTS

Triangle Illusions, 6

Chained Lightning, 11

Sound Waves, 23

Gypsy Wind, 27

Window to the World, 16

Stars & Diamonds, 40

Arabesque, 46

Diamonds in Light & Dark, 54

Casablanca, 35

Well-Connected Stars, 61

Polka-Dot Party, 68

String Stars, 72

Triangle Illusions

DESIGN BY CONNIE KAUFFMAN

Complementary colors like the blue and yellow scraps used in this runner are perfect fabric combinations.

Project Specifications

Skill Level: Beginner
Runner Size: 36" x 18"
Block Size: 9" x 9"
Number of Blocks: 3

Materials List

- Assorted blue scraps
- Assorted yellow scraps
- Backing 42" x 24"
- Batting 42" x 24"
- All-purpose thread to match fabrics
- Quilting thread
- 20 pieces 8½" x 11" paper
- Basic sewing tools and supplies

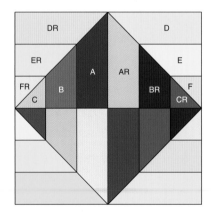

Triangle Illusions
9" x 9" Block
Make 3

Cutting

Note: *Choose scraps that are slightly larger than the largest piece to be cut.*

1. From assorted blue scraps, cut 28 each of 2" x 6" A rectangles, 2" x 4½" B rectangles and 3" C squares.

2. From assorted yellow scraps, cut 12 each of 2" x 6" D rectangles, 2" x 4½" E rectangles and 3" F squares.

Completing the Illusions Units

1. Set machine to a small stitch length to make removal of paper easier.

2. Prepare copies of full-size paper-piecing patterns.

3. To complete one unit, select one each A, B and C piece.

4. Place piece A right side up on the unmarked side of the paper, covering the piece A section and extending ¼" into all surrounding sections. Place piece B right sides together with piece A on the A-B seam side as shown in Figure 1; turn paper over and stitch on the marked A-B line.

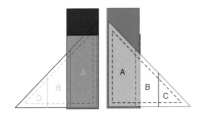

Figure 1

5. Press B to the right side as shown in Figure 2.

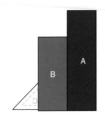

Figure 2

6. Repeat steps 3–5 with C to complete one A-B-C unit; repeat to make 14 A-B-C units.

7. Trim finished foundation along outside-edge line to complete the units.

8. Repeat steps 3–7 to complete 14 reverse A-B-C units and six each D-E-F and reverse D-E-F units referring to Figure 3.

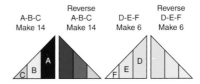

Figure 3

Completing the Triangle Illusions Blocks

1. Sew an A-B-C unit to a reverse D-E-F unit to make a corner unit as shown in Figure 4; repeat to make six corner units. Sew a reverse A-B-C unit to a D-E-F unit to make a reverse corner unit, again referring to Figure 4; repeat to make six reverse corner units. Press seams in one direction.

2. Join two corner units as shown in Figure 5 to make a row; press seam in one direction. Repeat to make two rows.

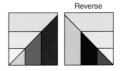

Figure 4

3. Join the two rows to complete one Triangle Illusions block; press seam in one direction. Repeat steps 2 and 3 to complete three blocks.

Figure 5

Completing the Quilt

1. Join the three blocks to complete the pieced center; press seams in one direction.

2. Join one A-B-C unit and one reverse A-B-C unit as shown in Figure 6 to make a side unit; press seam in one direction. Repeat to make eight side units.

Figure 6

3. Sew three side units to opposite long sides and one to each end of the pieced center referring to the Placement Diagram for positioning; press seams toward side units.

4. Carefully remove all paper.

5. Place the batting on a flat surface with backing right side up on top; place the pieced top right sides together with the backing/batting layers and pin to hold flat.

6. With the pieced top on the top, stitch all around ¼" from the edge of the pieced top, leaving a 6" opening on one side; trim excess batting and backing even with the edges of the pieced top. Trim batting layer even closer to the seam.

7. Turn right side out through the opening; press edges flat.

8. Hand-stitch opening closed; topstitch ¼" from edges all around.

9. Quilt as desired by hand or machine to finish. ♦

Triangle Illusions
Placement Diagram 36" x 18"

Reverse Paper-Piecing Pattern
Make 20 copies

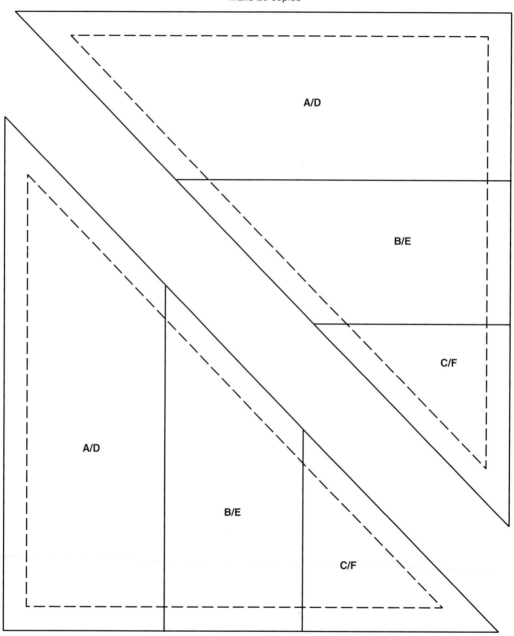

A/D

B/E

C/F

A/D

B/E

C/F

Paper-Piecing Pattern
Make 20 copies

Chained Lightning

DESIGN BY PAT CAMPBELL

The white background of this runner ties all the
scrap pieces together.

Project Specifications

Skill Level: Beginner
Runner Size: 40" x 16"
Block Size: 12" x 12"
Number of Blocks: 3

Materials

- Scraps dark fabrics
- ¼ yard dark fabric for binding
- 1 yard white solid
- Backing 46" x 22"
- Batting 46" x 22"
- Neutral-color all-purpose thread
- Quilting thread
- Basic sewing tools and supplies

Chained Lightning
12" x 12" Block
Make 3

Cutting

1. Make 12 photocopies of the foundation pattern.

2. Cut three 2¼" by fabric width strips dark fabric for binding.

3. Cut two 2½" x 36½" A strips and two 2½" x 16½" B strips from white solid.

4. Referring to the foundation paper and using dark scraps and white solid, cut pieces at least ¼" larger all around than corresponding spaces on the foundation pattern.

Completing the Blocks

1. Pin piece 1 to the unmarked side of a foundation pattern to cover the number 1 space.

2. Pin piece 2 to piece 1 with right sides together referring to Figure 1.

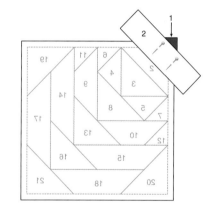

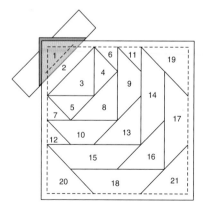

Figure 1

3. Turn paper over and stitch on the line between pieces 1 and 2, again referring to Figure 1.

4. Turn paper over, trim seam to ¼" and press piece 2 to the right side as shown in Figure 2.

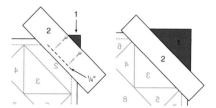

Figure 2

5. Continue to add pieces in numerical order, referring to foundation pattern for color, to make one unit.

6. Repeat to make 12 units.

7. Trim excess fabrics even with outside solid line of foundation papers as shown in Figure 3.

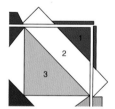

Figure 3

8. Arrange four units as shown in Figure 4. Join two units and press; repeat. Join the pieced units to complete one block; repeat to make three blocks.

Figure 4

9. Join the blocks to complete the pieced center. Press seams in one direction.

Completing the Runner

1. Sew an A strip to opposite long sides and a B strip to opposite short ends of the pieced center; press seams toward strips.

2. Carefully remove paper backing from all pieces.

3. Layer, quilt and bind referring to Finishing Your Quilt on page 80. ♦

Chained Lightning
Placement Diagram 40" x 16"

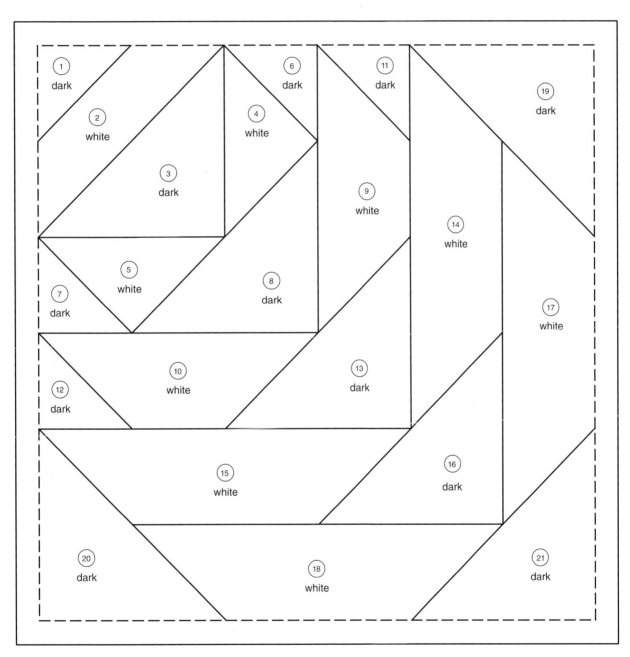

Foundation Pattern
Make 12 copies

Window to the World

DESIGN BY CHERYL ADAM FOR WESTMINSTER FIBERS

Bright-color blade shapes stand out
when appliquéd to a black background.

Project Specifications

Skill Level: Intermediate
Quilt Size: 40" diameter

Materials

- 7" x 7" square multicolored print* for C
- ½ yard green fan print*
- 1⅛ yards each blue and red fan prints*
- 1¾ yards black solid
- Backing 46" x 46"
- Thin cotton batting 46" x 46"
- Neutral-color all-purpose thread
- Clear nylon monofilament
- Quilting thread
- Freezer paper
- Tracing paper
- Basic sewing tools and supplies

Cutting

1. Cut a 40½" circle for the background D piece from black solid using a length of string tied to a pencil as shown in Figure 1. **Note:** *The string should measure 20¼" from the center to the pencil.*

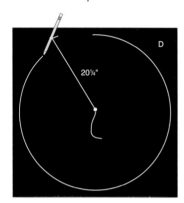

Figure 1

2. Cut 2¼"-wide bias strips from black solid to total 140" for binding.

3. Prepare templates using patterns given; cut as directed on each piece, adding a ¼" seam allowance all around when cutting fabric shapes.

Completing the Quilt

1. Center and pin each freezer-paper shape shiny side up on the wrong side of each corresponding fabric shape as shown in Figure 2.

Figure 2

2. Turn the seam allowance edges over the edges of the freezer-paper shapes of C and each A piece all around, again referring to Figure 2; press the tip of iron just over the seam allowance to the freezer paper to hold.

3. Repeat step 2 on the straight sides of B, leaving the curved edge unfolded as shown in Figure 3.

Figure 3

4. Fold the D background piece in half, and then quarters and then eighths as shown in Figure 4; press to make creases.

Figure 4

5. Center and pin or baste the C circle to the D background.

6. Using clear nylon monofilament, stitch C in place with a machine blind hemstitch. **Note:** *Sew a test sample to determine the stitch length and width to use.*

7. Referring to Figure 5, center and pin or baste blue A pieces on the half and quarter creased lines, and red A pieces on the eighth creased lines, leaving ⅛" between end of A and the stitched C piece as shown in Figure 5.

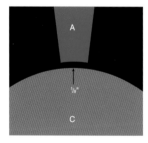

Figure 5

8. Pin one each red and blue A pieces between the pinned or basted A pieces, leaving ⅛" between pieces and referring to the Placement Diagram for positioning. When pleased with positioning of all A pieces, stitch in place as in step 6.

9. Insert the B pieces between the A points, leaving ⅛" between pieces; stitch in place as in step 6 to complete the stitched top.

10. When all pieces have been appliquéd, carefully cut a slit in the background behind each piece and remove the freezer-paper shapes.

11. Layer, quilt and bind referring to Finishing Your Quilt on page 80. ♦

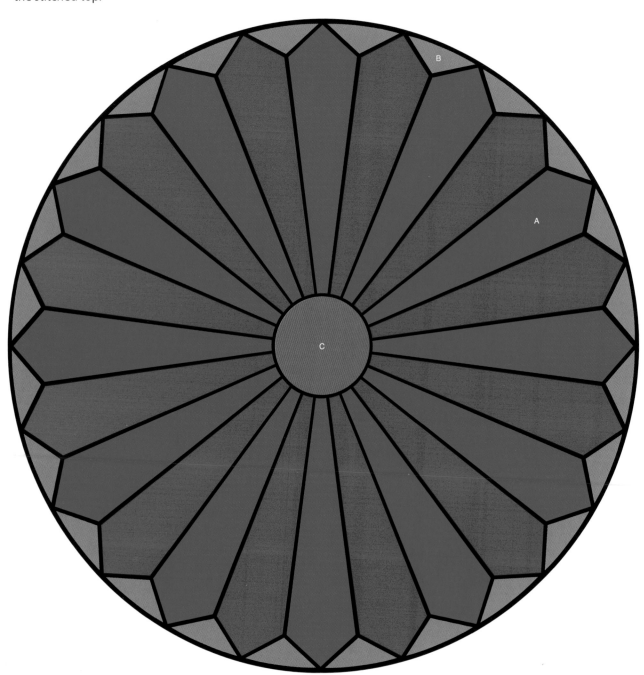

Window Westminster Fibers
Placement Diagram 40" diameter

Add a ¼" seam allowance all around
each shape when cutting fabric pieces.

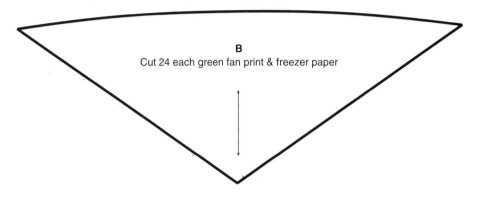

B
Cut 24 each green fan print & freezer paper

Add a ¼" seam allowance all around
each shape when cutting fabric pieces.

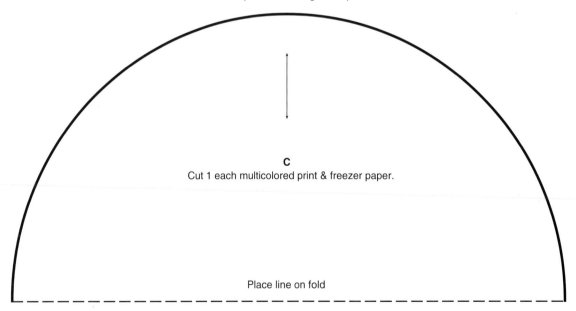

C
Cut 1 each multicolored print & freezer paper.

Place line on fold

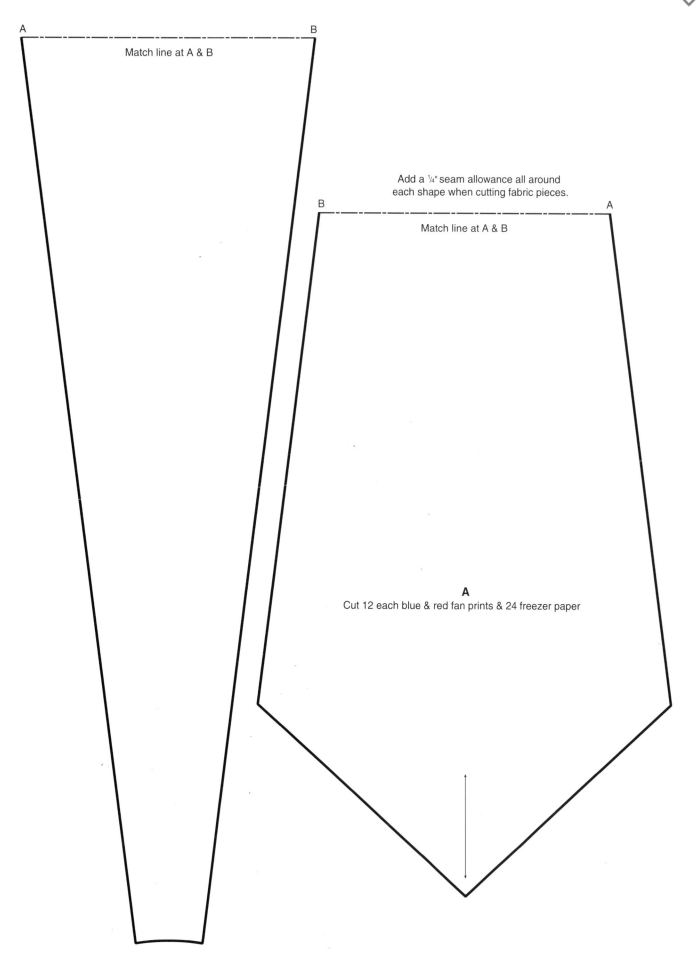

A   B

Match line at A & B

Add a ¼" seam allowance all around
each shape when cutting fabric pieces.

B   A

Match line at A & B

A
Cut 12 each blue & red fan prints & 24 freezer paper

Sound Waves

DESIGN BY FLORENCE HARSCHE OF FLORENCE'S CREATIONS

Just like real sound waves, the pieces in this design look like they reverberate or vibrate.

Project Specifications

Skill Level: Intermediate
Quilt Size: 33½" x 33½"
Block Size: 6" x 6"
Number of Blocks: 16

Materials

- ⅜ yard pink/orange mottled
- ½ yard teal mottled
- 1 yard multicolored metallic mottles
- 1⅜ yards black tonal
- Backing 40" x 40"
- Batting 40" x 40"
- Neutral-color all-purpose thread
- Quilting thread
- Paper
- Basic sewing tools and supplies

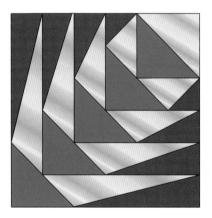

Sound Waves
6" x 6" Block
Make 16

Cutting

1. Cut four 2¼" x 36" A strips from pink/orange mottled.

2. Cut four 3¼" by fabric width strips from teal mottled; subcut strips into 40 (3¼") squares. Cut each square in half on one diagonal to make 80 triangles for pieces 2, 7, 12, 17 and 22.

3. Cut one 3¼" by fabric width strip from multicolored metallic mottled; subcut strip into eight 3¼" squares. Cut each square on one diagonal to make 16 triangles for piece 1.

4. Cut 12 (1¾" by fabric width) strips from multicolored metallic mottled; subcut strips into 32 each 4" strips for pieces 8 and 9, 5" strips for pieces 13 and 14 and 6" strips for pieces 18 and 19.

5. Cut two 2⅝" by fabric width strips from multicolored metallic mottled; subcut strips into 16 (2⅝") squares. Cut each square in half on one diagonal to make 32 triangles for pieces 3 and 4.

6. Cut one 2¼" by fabric width strip from black tonal; subcut strip into 16 (2¼") squares. Cut each square in half on one diagonal to make 32 triangles for pieces 5 and 6.

7. Cut 10 (1¾" by fabric width) strips from black tonal; subcut strips into 32 each 3" strips for pieces 10 and 11, 4" strips for pieces 15 and 16 and 5" strips for pieces 20 and 21.

8. Cut four 3½" x 36" B strips from black tonal.

9. Cut four 2¼" by fabric width strips from black tonal for binding.

Completing the Blocks

1. Prepare 16 copies of the paper-piecing pattern.

2. Place piece 1 right side up on the unmarked side of the paper, covering section 1 and extending at least ¼" into all surrounding areas. Place piece 2 right sides together with piece 1 on the 1-2 seam side as shown in Figure 1; turn paper over and stitch on the marked 1-2 line, again referring to Figure 1.

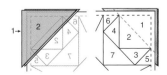

Figure 1

3. Trim excess seam allowance to extend ¼" beyond the 1-2 line; press piece 2 to the right side as shown in Figure 2.

Figure 2

4. Continue adding pieces in numerical order in this manner until entire paper foundation is covered.

5. Trim finished foundation along outside-edge line to complete one Sound Waves block.

6. Repeat steps 2–5 to complete 16 blocks.

Completing the Quilt

1. Join four Sound Waves blocks to make a row as shown in Figure 3; press seams in one direction. Repeat to make four rows.

Make 4

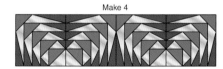

Figure 3

2. Join the rows referring to the Placement Diagram to complete the pieced top; press seams in one direction.

3. Sew an A strip to a B strip with right sides together along length; press seams toward B strips. Repeat to make four A-B strips.

4. Center and sew an A-B strip to each side of the pieced center, stopping stitching ¼" from each end, as shown in Figure 4.

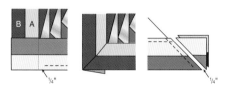

Figure 4

5. Miter corners, matching A-B seams, again referring to Figure 4; trim seam allowance to ¼" and press seams open to complete the pieced top. Remove paper patterns.

6. Layer, quilt and bind referring to Finishing Your Quilt on page 80. ♦

Sound Waves
Placement Diagram 33¹/₂" x 33¹/₂"

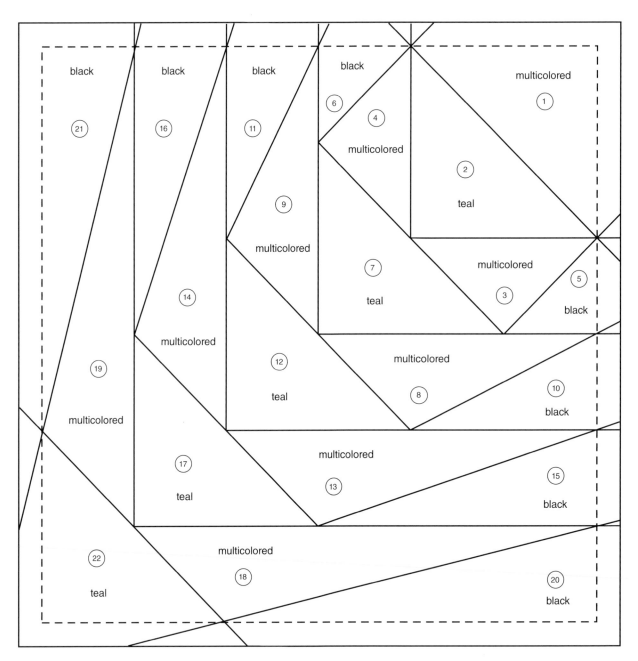

Paper-Piecing Pattern
Make 16 copies

Gypsy Wind

DESIGN BY PHYLLIS DOBBS

Add pieced borders to two sides only to create a unique quilt.

Project Specifications

Skill Level: Beginner
Quilt Size: 45" x 53"

Materials

- ¼ yard light turquoise tonal
- ¼ yard medium green tonal
- ⅓ yard small turquoise print
- ⅜ yard multicolored medallion stripe
- ½ yard medium turquoise tonal
- ⅝ yard small turquoise medallion print
- ¾ yard purple print
- ¾ yard large multicolored print
- 1¼ yards light green tonal
- Batting 51" x 59"
- Backing 51" x 59"
- All-purpose thread to match fabrics
- Quilting thread
- Basic sewing tools and supplies

Cutting

1. Cut one 5½" by fabric width strip light turquoise tonal; subcut strip into two 5½" A squares.

2. Cut one 5½" by fabric width strip medium turquoise tonal; subcut strip into two 5½" B squares.

3. Cut two 1½" x 38½" M strips and two 1½" x 32½" N strips medium turquoise tonal.

4. Cut one 5⅞" by fabric width strip light green tonal; subcut strip into four 5⅞" squares. Cut each square in half on one diagonal to make eight C triangles.

5. Cut two 2" x 30½" G strips light green tonal.

6. Cut two 4⅞" by fabric width strips light green tonal; subcut strips into 10 (4⅞") squares. Cut each square in half on one diagonal to make 20 P triangles.

7. Cut one 4½" by fabric width strip light green tonal; subcut strip into four 4½" R squares.

8. Cut five 2¼" by fabric width strips light green tonal for binding.

9. Cut one 5⅞" by fabric width strip purple print; subcut strip into six 5⅞" squares. Cut each square in half on one diagonal to make 12 D triangles.

10. Cut two 4⅞" by fabric width strips purple print; subcut strips into 10 (4⅞") squares. Cut each square in half on one diagonal to make 20 Q triangles.

11. Cut one 6¼" by fabric width strip purple print; subcut strip into three 6¼" squares. Cut each square on both diagonals to make 12 J triangles.

12. Cut one 5½" by fabric width strip large multicolored print; subcut strip into seven 5½" E squares.

13. Cut one 5⅞" by fabric width strip large multicolored print; subcut strip into two 5⅞" squares and one 5½" E square (to total eight with squares cut in step 12). Cut the two 5⅞" squares in half on one diagonal to make four F triangles.

14. Cut two 4½" x 30½" L strips large multicolored print.

15. Cut two 1½" x 30½" H strips medium green tonal.

16. Cut one 3" by fabric width strip medium green tonal; subcut strip into four 3" U squares.

17. Cut one 6¼" by fabric width strip small turquoise print; subcut strip into three 6¼" squares and two 3⅜" squares. Cut the larger squares on both diagonals to make 12 I triangles (discard two) and the smaller squares in half on one diagonal to make four K triangles.

18. Cut two 3" x 40½" S strips small turquoise medallion print.

19. Cut three 3" by fabric width T strips small turquoise medallion print.

20. Cut two 4½" x 32½" O strips multicolored medallion stripe with large medallions centered.

Completing the Top

1. Sew an A square to a B square; repeat. Press seams toward B.

2. Join the A-B units to complete the center unit; press seam in one direction.

3. Sew C to D along the diagonal to make a C-D unit; press seam toward D. Repeat to make eight C-D units.

4. Join two C-D units as shown in Figure 1; press seam in one direction. Repeat to make four side units.

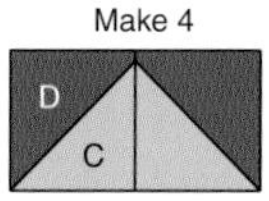

Make 4

Figure 1

5. Sew a side unit to opposite sides of the center unit as shown in Figure 2; press seams toward the center unit.

Figure 2

Make 2

Figure 3

6. Sew E to each end of the two remaining side units as shown in Figure 3; press seams toward E. Sew these units to the top and bottom of the center unit as shown in Figure 4; press seams away from the center unit.

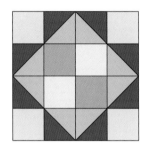

Figure 4

7. Sew D to F along the diagonal to make a D-F unit; press seam toward D. Repeat to make four D-F units.

8. Join two E squares with two D-F units to complete a D-F-E strip as shown in Figure 5; press seams toward E squares. Repeat to make two D-F-E strips.

Make 2

Figure 5

9. Sew a D-F-E strip to opposite sides of the pieced center unit as shown in Figure 6 to complete the pieced center; press seams toward the D-F-E strips.

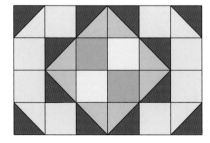

Figure 6

10. Sew a G strip and then an H strip to the top and bottom of the pieced center; press seams toward G and then H.

11. Sew I to J as shown in Figure 7; press seam toward J. Repeat to make 10 I-J units.

Figure 7

12. Join five I-J units, one J triangle and two K triangles, as shown in Figure 8, to make an I-J-K strip; press seams in one direction. Repeat to make two I-J-K strips.

Make 2

Figure 8

13. Sew an I-J-K strip to the top and bottom of the pieced center referring to the Placement Diagram for positioning; press seams toward H strips.

14. Sew an L strip to the top and bottom of the pieced center; press seams toward L strips.

15. Sew an M strip to opposite long sides and N strips to the top and bottom of the pieced center; press seams toward M and N strips.

16. Sew an O strip to the top and bottom of the pieced center; press seams toward N strips.

17. Sew P to Q along the diagonal to make a P-Q unit; press seam toward Q. Repeat to make 20 P-Q units.

18. Join two P-Q units as shown in Figure 9 to make a side unit; press seam in one direction. Repeat to make 10 side units.

Make 10

Figure 9

19. Join five side units with two R squares to make a side strip referring to the Placement Diagram for positioning; press seams toward R and then in one direction. Repeat to make two side strips.

20. Sew a side strip to opposite sides of the pieced center referring to the Placement Diagram for positioning; press seams toward M strips.

21. Sew an S strip to the top and bottom of the pieced center; press seams toward S strips.

22. Join the T strips on short ends to make one long strip; press seams open. Subcut strip into two 48½" T strips.

23. Sew a U square to each end of each T strip; press seams toward T strips.

24. Sew a T-U strip to opposite long sides of the pieced center; press seams toward the T-U strip to complete the pieced top.

25. Layer, quilt and bind referring to Finishing Your Quilt on page 80. ♦

Gypsy Wind
Placement Diagram 45" x 53"

Casablanca

DESIGN BY SUSAN KNAPP

The use of batiks in lights, mediums and darks creates a design that is both mysterious and compelling.

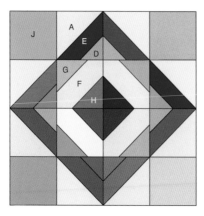

Medium-Corner Casablanca
12" x 12" Block
Make 6

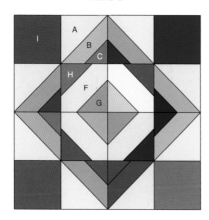

Dark-Corner Casablanca
12" x 12" Block
Make 6

Project Specifications

Skill Level: Intermediate
Quilt Size: 44" x 56"
Block Size: 12" x 12"
Number of Blocks: 12

Materials

- 6 fat quarters light-color batiks
- 6 fat quarters medium-color batiks
- 6 fat quarters dark-color batiks
- ⅓ yard cream batik
- ⅝ yard black batik
- Batting 52" x 64"
- Backing 52" x 64"
- All-purpose thread to match fabrics
- Quilting thread
- Basic sewing tools and supplies

Cutting

1. Cut two 3⅞" x 21" strips from each of the light-color fat quarters; subcut strips into eight 3⅞" squares each fabric. Cut each square in half on one diagonal to make 96 A triangles.

2. Cut two 3½" x 21" strips from each of the light-color fat quarters; subcut strips into eight 3½" F squares each fabric.

3. Cut two 3½" x 21" strips from each of the medium- and dark-color fat quarters; set aside one of each for M strips. Subcut each of the remaining strips into four 3½" J squares and one 2¾" G square; subcut each remaining dark-color strip into four 3½" I squares and one 2¾" H square.

4. Cut one 3⅞" x 21" strip from each of the medium- and dark-color fat quarters; subcut each strip into four 3⅞" squares. Cut each square in half on one diagonal to make 48 each medium B and dark E triangles.

5. Cut one 2¾" x 21" strip from each of the medium- and dark-color fat quarters; subcut each medium-color strip into seven 2¾" G squares and each dark-color strip into seven 2¾" H squares.

6. Cut one 2" x 21" strip from each of the medium- and dark-color fat quarters; subcut each medium-color strip into eight 2" D squares and each dark-color strip into eight 2" C squares.

7. Cut two 1½" x 36½" K strips cream batik.

8. Cut three 1½" by fabric width L strips cream batik.

9. Cut six 2¼" by fabric width strips black batik for binding.

Completing the Blocks

1. Sew a light A to a medium B along the diagonal to make an A-B unit as shown in Figure 1; do not press. Repeat to make 48 A-B units.

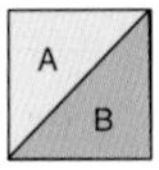

Figure 1

2. Draw a diagonal line from corner to corner on the wrong side of each C square.

3. Place a C square right sides together on the B corner of an A-B unit and stitch on the marked line as shown in Figure 2; trim seam to ¼" to complete an A-B-C unit as shown in Figure 3. Repeat to make 48 A-B-C units.

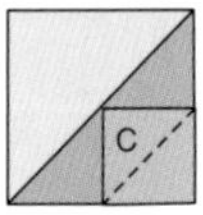

Figure 2

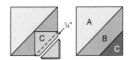

Figure 3

4. Press seams on 24 A-B-C units toward A and on the remaining 24 units toward C as shown in Figure 4.

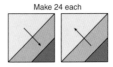

Make 24 each

Figure 4

5. Repeat steps 1–3 with A, E and D pieces referring to Figure 5; press seams as in step 4 and referring to Figure 6.

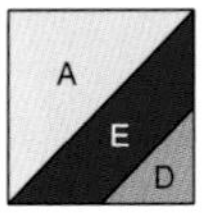

Figure 5

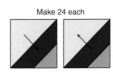

Make 24 each

Figure 6

6. Draw a diagonal line from corner to corner on the wrong side of each G and H square.

7. Place a G square right sides together on one corner of F; stitch on the marked line as shown in Figure 7; trim seam to ¼". Repeat with H on the opposite corner of F referring to Figure 8 to complete one F-G-H unit. Repeat to make 48 F-G-H units.

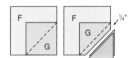

Figure 7

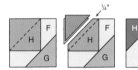

Figure 8

8. Press seams on 24 F-G-H units toward G, and on the remaining 24 units toward H as shown in Figure 9.

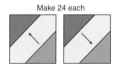

Make 24 each

Figure 9

9. For each Dark-Corner Casablanca block, arrange eight A-B-C units and four F-G-H units in rows with four I squares, placing the units with seams pressed in the direction of the arrows as shown in Figure 10.

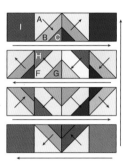

Figure 10

10. Join the units in rows as arranged; pressing seams in the direction of the arrows in between each row as shown in Figure 10. Join the rows and press in the direction of the outer arrows as shown in Figure 10 to complete a Dark-Corner Casablanca block. Repeat to make six blocks.

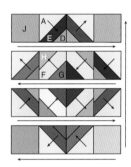

Figure 11

11. Repeat steps 9 and 10 with eight A-E-D units, four F-G-H units and four J squares to complete a Medium-Corner Casablanca block as shown in Figure 11. Repeat to make six blocks.

Completing the Quilt

1. Join two Medium-Corner Casablanca blocks with one Dark-Corner Casablanca block to make an X row as shown in Figure 12; press seams in one direction. Repeat to make two X rows.

X Row
Make 2

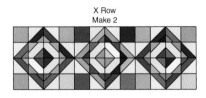

Y Row
Make 2

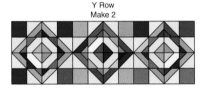

Figure 12

2. Join two Dark-Corner Casablanca blocks with one Medium-Corner Casablanca block to make a Y row, again referring to Figure 12; press seams in one direction. Repeat to make two Y rows.

3. Alternate and join rows with seams in adjoining rows pressed in opposite directions to complete the pieced center; press seams in one direction.

4. Sew a K strip to the top and bottom of the pieced center; press seams toward K strips.

5. Join the L strips on short ends to make one long strip; press seams open. Subcut strip into two 50½" L strips.

6. Sew L strips to opposite long sides of the pieced center; press seams toward L strips.

7. Trim the M strips to 17½"; determine placement around edges and join on the short ends in sets of three to make four M borders.

8. Fold each M border in half along width and crease to mark the center; repeat with the pieced center.

9. Matching the creases, sew an M border to opposite sides of the pieced center; trim excess at each end even with the pieced center and press seams toward M borders.

10. Repeat step 9 with M borders on the top and bottom of the pieced center to complete the pieced top.

11. Layer, quilt and bind referring to Finishing Your Quilt on page 80. ♦

Casablanca
Placement Diagram 44" x 56"

Stars & Diamonds

DESIGN BY JANICE MCKEE

Any color of fabric may be used to make this quilt; the only requirement is that there be true value changes from light to medium to dark.

Project Notes:

Before you start, divide your scraps into three stacks and estimate the amount of fabric in each pile. The Materials list gives approximate amounts of light, medium and dark fabric needed. If you need more fabric of a certain value, treat yourself to a few fat quarters. The scrappier this quilt is, the better.

Project Specifications

Skill Level: Intermediate
Quilt Size: 59" x 59"
Block Size: 12" x 12"
Number of Blocks: 16

Materials

- ⅔ yard dark scraps
- 1¼ yards medium scraps
- 1¾ yards navy print for borders
- 2 yards light scraps
- Backing 65" x 65"
- Batting 65" x 65"
- 7 yards self-made or purchased binding
- Neutral-color all-purpose thread
- Water-erasable marker
- Basic sewing tools and supplies

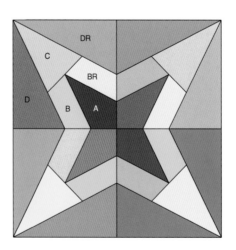

Stars & Diamonds
12" x 12" Block
Make 16

Cutting

1. Prepare templates using pattern pieces. Cut as directed on each piece for one block.

2. Repeat and cut pieces for 16 separate blocks. ***Note:*** *Keep the pieces for each block together by placing them in a plastic bag.*

3. Cut four E strips navy print 6" x 59½" along fabric length.

Assembly

1. To piece one block, sew B and BR to A; add C, D and DR referring to Figure 1; repeat for four units.

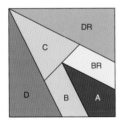

Figure 1

2. Join four units to complete one block as shown in Figure 2; repeat for 16 blocks. Press, and if necessary, square up blocks to 12½" square.

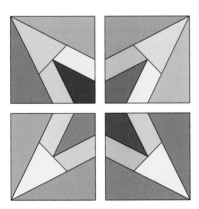

Figure 2

3. Arrange and sew blocks in four rows of four blocks each. Sew rows together to complete the pieced center, referring to the placement diagram. Press seams in one direction.

4. Sew an E border strip to each side of the pieced center, mitering corners; press seams toward strips.

5. Mark desired quilting design in border strips using water-erasable marker. Refer to Figure 3 for suggested quilting design for blocks.

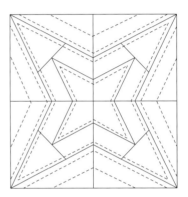

Figure 3

6. Layer, quilt and bind referring to Finishing Your Quilt on page 80. ♦

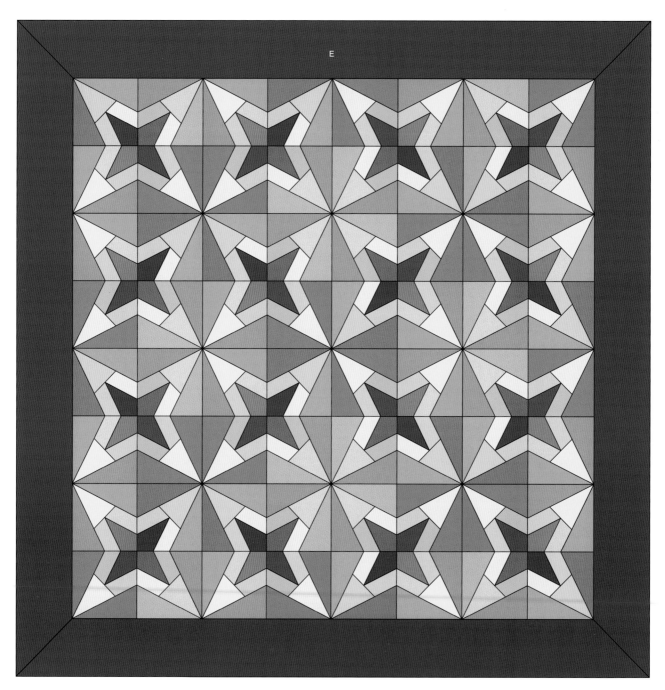

E

Stars & Diamonds
Placement Diagram 59" x 59"

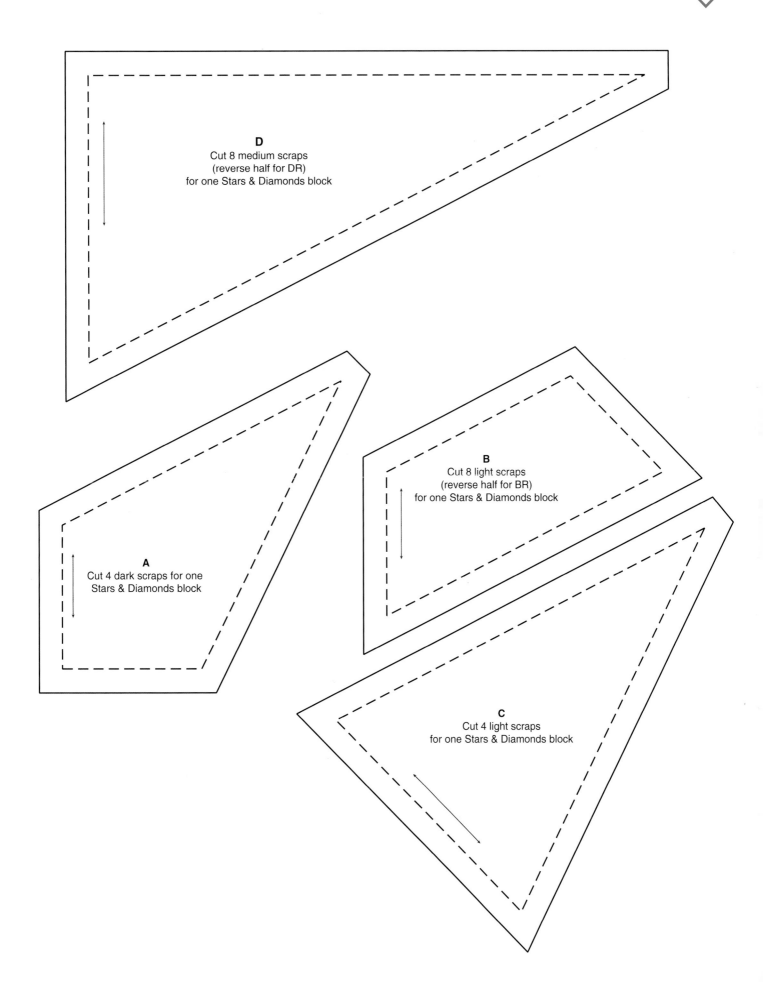

D
Cut 8 medium scraps
(reverse half for DR)
for one Stars & Diamonds block

A
Cut 4 dark scraps for one
Stars & Diamonds block

B
Cut 8 light scraps
(reverse half for BR)
for one Stars & Diamonds block

C
Cut 4 light scraps
for one Stars & Diamonds block

Arabesque

DESIGN BY LARISA KEY FOR CLASSIC COTTONS

A simple trick makes the curved piecing easy in this two-block combination lap quilt.

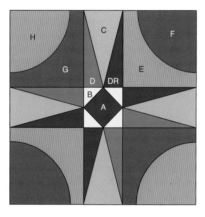

Arabesque
12" x 12" Block
Make 6

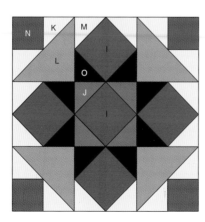

Five Spot
12" x 12" Block
Make 6

Project Specifications

Skill Level: Intermediate
Quilt Size: 46" x 58"
Block Size: 12" x 12"
Number of Blocks: 12

Materials

- ¼ yard brown print
- ⅜ yard orange/green check
- ½ yard orange/pink check
- ⅝ yard wine print
- ⅝ yard each green and yellow tonals
- ⅔ yard each pink tonal and black floral
- ¾ yard black tonal
- 1¼ yards red paisley
- Backing 52" x 64"
- Batting 52" x 64"
- Neutral-color all-purpose thread
- Quilting thread
- Template material
- ¾ yard fusible web
- Basic sewing tools and supplies

Cutting

1. Prepare templates for C and D using patterns given. Cut one 5¼" by fabric width strip each wine print and green tonal and two strips orange/pink check; place the C and D templates on the strips to cut pieces as shown in Figure 1 and as directed on the patterns for number to cut.

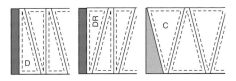

Figure 1

2. Mark a 7½"-diameter circle onto template material. Using template, trace six circle shapes onto the paper side of the fusible web. Cut out shapes, leaving a margin around each one.

3. Bond three circles onto the wrong side of the black floral F and pink tonal H; cut out shapes on the traced lines. Remove paper backing.

4. Cut three 10½" squares each pink tonal (E) and black floral (G).

5. Cut six 2¼" by fabric width strips black tonal for binding.

6. Cut three 2½" by fabric width strips each yellow and black tonals; subcut strips into 48 (2½") squares each yellow M and black tonal O. Draw a diagonal line from corner to corner on the wrong side of each square.

7. Cut two 2⅞" by fabric width strips yellow tonal; subcut strips into 24 (2⅞") squares. Cut each square in half on one diagonal to make 48 K triangles.

8. Cut one 1¾" by fabric width strip yellow tonal; subcut strip into 24 (1¾") B squares. Draw a diagonal line from corner to corner on the wrong side of each square.

9. Cut one 3" by fabric width strip wine print; subcut strip into six 3" A squares.

10. Cut five 1½" by fabric width strips wine print. Join strips on short ends to make one long strip; press seams open. Subcut strip into two 48½" P strips and two 38½" Q strips.

11. Cut four 4½" by fabric width strips red paisley; subcut strips into 30 (4½") I squares.

12. Cut five 4" by fabric width strips red paisley. Join strips on short ends to make one long strip; press seams open. Subcut strip into two 51½" T strips and two 46½" U strips.

13. Cut two 2½" by fabric width strips green tonal; subcut strips into 24 (2½") J squares. Draw a diagonal line from corner to corner on the wrong side of each square.

14. Cut five 1" by fabric width strips green tonal. Join strips on short ends to make one long strip; press seams open. Subcut strip into two 50½" R strips and two 39½" S strips.

15. Cut two 2½" by fabric width strips brown print; subcut strips into 24 (2½") N squares.

16. Cut two 4⅞" by fabric width strips orange/green check; subcut strips into 12 (4⅞") squares. Cut each square in half on one diagonal to make 24 L triangles.

Completing the Arabesque Blocks

1. Referring to Figure 2, place a B square right sides together on opposite corners of A; stitch on the marked lines.

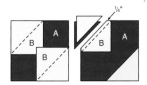

Figure 2

2. Trim seam allowance to ¼"; press B to the right side.

3. Repeat steps 1 and 2 on the remaining corners of A to complete an A-B unit as shown in Figure 3; repeat to make six A-B units.

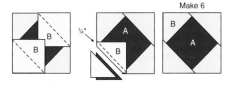

Figure 3

4. Fold and crease each F and H circle to mark the centers.

5. Fold and crease each E and G square to mark the centers.

6. Center and fuse an F circle to each E square and an H circle to each G square as shown in Figure 4.

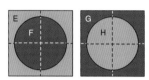

Figure 4

7. Machine zigzag-stitch around the edges of each F and H circle.

8. Cut the stitched units into quarters using creased lines as guides to yield four 5¼" units from each fused square as shown in Figure 5; there will be a total of 12 E-F units and 12 G-H units.

Figure 5

9. Sew a green D and a wine DR to C to make a C-D unit as shown in Figure 6; repeat to make 12 C-D units. Press seams away from C.

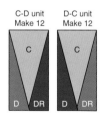

Figure 6

10. Sew a wine D and a green DR to C to make a D-C unit, again referring to Figure 6; repeat to make 12 D-C units. Press seams away from C.

11. To complete one Arabesque block, sew a C-D unit to opposite sides of an A-B unit to complete the center row as shown in Figure 7; press seams toward the A-B unit.

Figure 7

12. Sew a D-C unit between an E-F and G-H unit to complete one side row as shown in Figure 8; repeat to make a second side row.

Figure 8

13. Sew the center row between the two side rows as shown in Figure 9 to complete one Arabesque block; press seams away from the center row. Repeat steps 11–13 to make six blocks.

Figure 9

Completing the Five Spot Blocks

1. Repeat steps 1–3 for Completing the Arabesque Blocks to complete six I-J and 24 I-M-O units as shown in Figure 10.

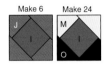

Make 6   Make 24

Figure 10

2. Sew K to two adjacent sides of N as shown in Figure 11; press seams toward N. Repeat to make 24 K-N units.

Make 24

Figure 11

3. Sew L to each K-N unit to complete 24 L-K-N units as shown in Figure 12; press seams toward L.

Make 24

Figure 12

4. To complete one Five Spot block, sew one I-J unit between two I-M-O units to make the center row as shown in Figure 13; press seams toward the I-J unit.

Figure 13

5. Sew an I-M-O unit between two L-K-N units to make the top row as shown in Figure 14; press seams toward the L-K-N units. Repeat to make the bottom row.

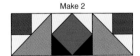

Make 2

Figure 14

6. Sew the center row between the top and bottom rows to complete one Five Spot block as shown in Figure 15; press seams away from the center row. Repeat steps 4–6 to make six blocks.

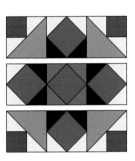

Figure 15

Completing the Quilt

1. Sew one Five Spot block between two Arabesque blocks to make an X row as shown in Figure 16; press seams toward the Five Spot block. Repeat to make two X rows.

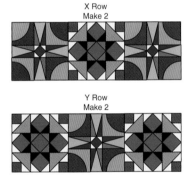

X Row
Make 2

Y Row
Make 2

Figure 16

2. Sew one Arabesque block between two Five Spot blocks to make a Y row, again referring to Figure 16; press seams toward the Five Spot blocks. Repeat to make two Y rows.

3. Referring to the Placement Diagram for placement, join the X and Y rows to complete the pieced center; press seams in one direction.

4. Sew the border strips to sides first and then top and bottom in alphabetical order, referring to the Placement Diagram for positioning, to complete the pieced top; press seams toward strips as added.

5. Layer, quilt and bind referring to Finishing Your Quilt on page 80. ♦

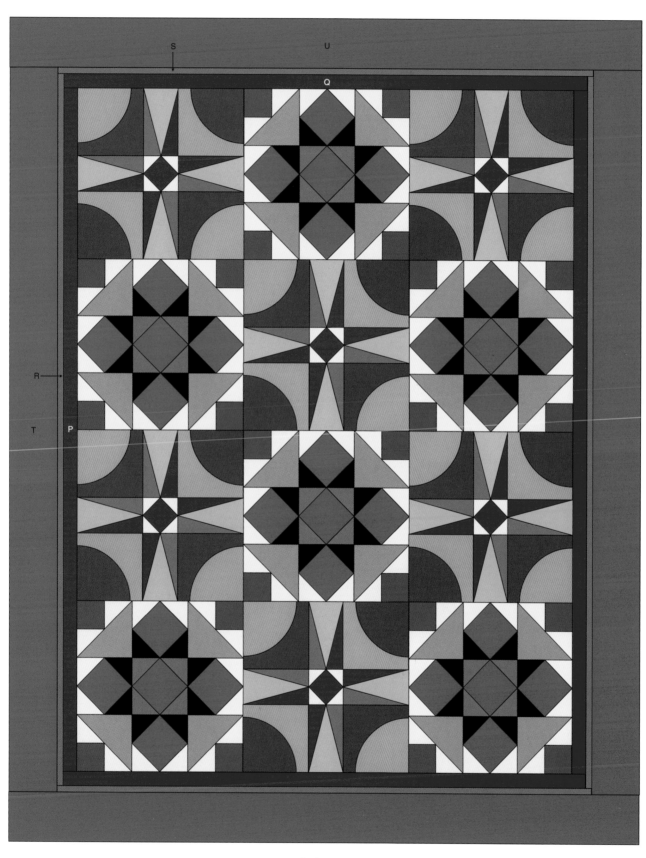

Arabesque
Placement Diagram 46" x 58"

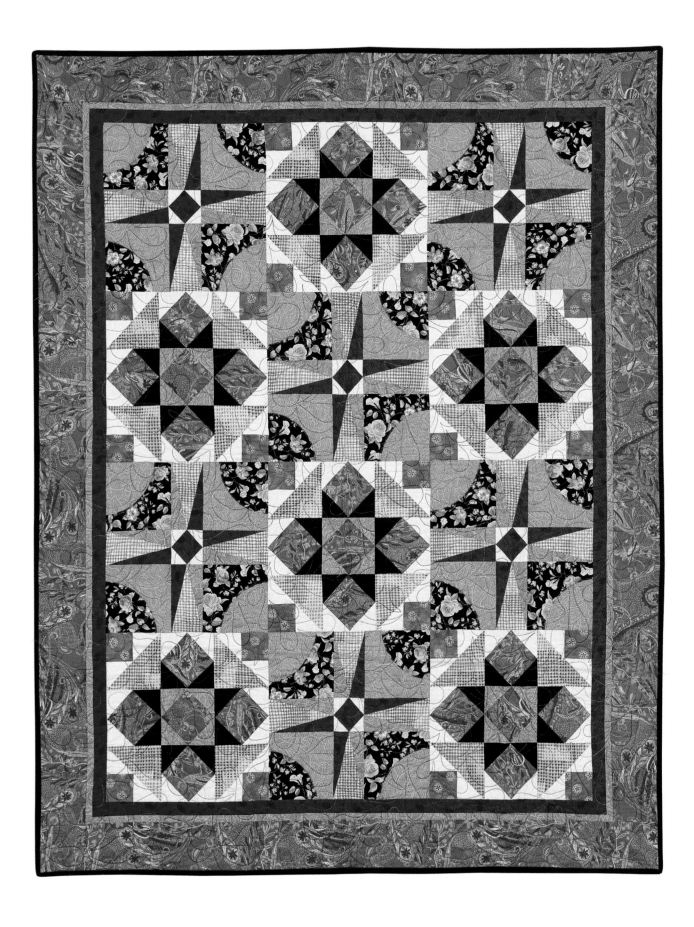

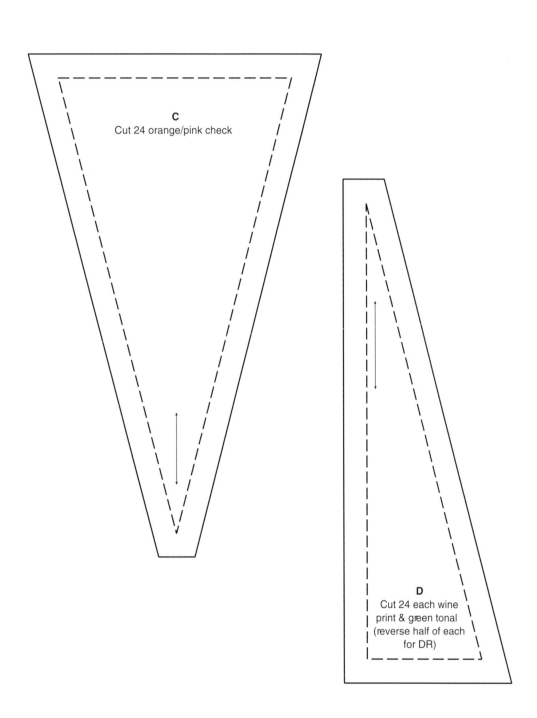

C
Cut 24 orange/pink check

D
Cut 24 each wine
print & green tonal
(reverse half of each
for DR)

Diamonds in Light & Dark

DESIGN BY GINA GEMPESAW QUILTED BY CAROLE WHALING

Create depth and interest with a limited color palette.
One block made with two combinations produces
amazing results

Project Specifications

Skill Level: Confident Beginner
Quilt Size: 56" x 74"
Block Size: 9" x 9"
Number of Blocks: 35

Materials

- ½ yard carbon string necklace print
- ⅞ yard green/blue fan print
- ⅞ yard green line tonal
- 2⅛ yards white solid
- 2⅛ yards green diamond carbon print
- Backing 64" x 82"
- Batting 64" x 82"
- Neutral-color all-purpose thread
- Basic sewing tools and supplies

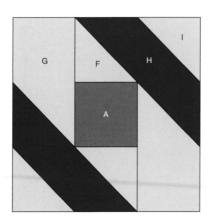

Blue Diamond
9" x 9" Block
Make 17

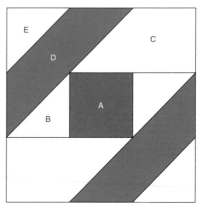

Green Diamond
9" x 9" Block
Make 18

Cutting

1. From carbon string necklace print, cut three 3½" by fabric width strips; subcut strips into 35 (3½") A squares.

2. Cut one 3" by fabric width strip of carbon string necklace print; subcut strip into eight 3″ x 5″ P rectangles.

3. From green/blue fan print, cut three 6⅞" by fabric width strips; subcut strips into 17 (6⅞") squares. Cut each square in half on one diagonal to make 34 H triangles.

4. Cut one 3" by fabric width strip green/blue fan print; subcut into eight 3" x 5" O rectangles.

5. From green line tonal, cut three 6⅞" by fabric width strips; subcut strips into 18 (6⅞") squares. Cut each square in half on one diagonal to make 36 D triangles.

6. Cut one 3" by fabric width strip green line tonal; subcut into eight 3" x 5" N rectangles

7. From white solid, cut two 3⅞" by fabric width strips; subcut into 18 (3⅞") squares. Cut each square in half on one diagonal to make 36 B triangles.

8. Cut three 6⅞" by fabric width strips white solid; subcut into 36 (3½" x 6⅞") C rectangles.

9. Cut three 3½" by fabric width strips white solid; subcut into 36 (3½") E squares.

10. Cut one 5" by fabric width strip white solid; subcut into four 5" R squares

11. Cut three 5" by fabric width L strips white solid.

12. Cut two 5" x 27½" Q strips white solid.

13. From green diamond carbon print, cut two 3⅞" by fabric width strips; subcut into 17 (3⅞") squares. Cut each square on one diagonal to make 34 F triangles.

14. Cut three 6⅞" by fabric width strips green diamond carbon print; subcut into 34 (3½" x 6⅞") G rectangles.

15. Cut three 3½" by fabric width strips green diamond carbon print; subcut into 34 (3½") I squares.

16. Cut one 3" by fabric width strip green diamond carbon print; subcut into eight 3" x 5" M rectangles.

17. Cut six 1½" by fabric width J/K strips green diamond carbon print.

18. Cut seven 2¼" by fabric width strips green diamond carbon print for binding.

Completing the Green Diamond Blocks

1. Lay the C rectangles right side up on a flat surface and cut one end of each rectangle at a 45-degree angle as shown in Figure 1. **Note:** *Be sure all C rectangles are cut the same way.*

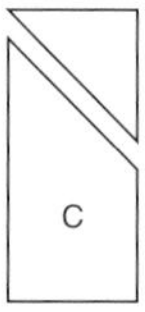

Figure 1

2. Draw a diagonal line from corner to corner on the wrong side of each E square.

3. Place an E square on the 90-degree corner of D and stitch on the marked line as shown in Figure 2; trim seam to ¼" and press E to the right side to complete a D-E unit, again referring to Figure 2.

Figure 2

4. Repeat step 3 to complete a total of 36 D-E units.

5. To complete one Green Diamond block, sew B to opposite sides of A, as shown in Figure 3, to make an A-B unit; press seams toward A.

Figure 3

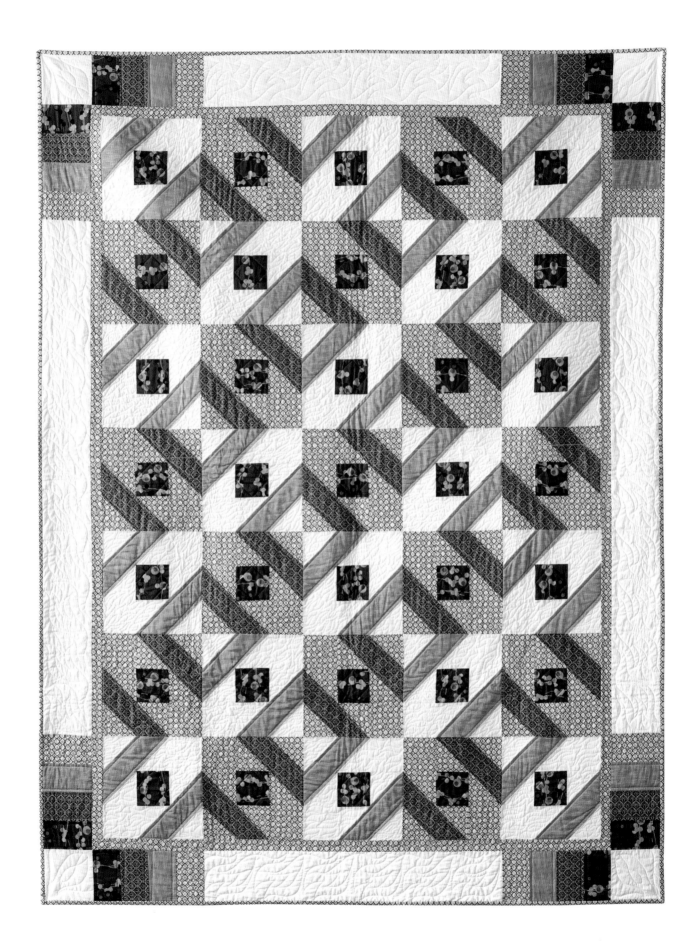

6. Sew C to opposite long sides of the A-B unit, as shown in Figure 4, to make an A-B-C unit; press seams toward C.

Figure 4

7. Sew a D-E unit to opposite sides of the A-B-C unit to complete one block as shown in Figure 5; press seams toward the D-E units.

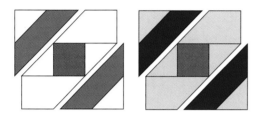

Figure 5

8. Repeat steps 5–7 to complete a total of 18 Green Diamond blocks.

Completing the Blue Diamond Blocks

1. Lay the G rectangles right side up on a flat surface and cut one end of each rectangle at a 45-degree angle as shown in Figure 6. **Note:** *Be sure all G rectangles are cut the same way.*

Figure 6

2. Draw a diagonal line from corner to corner on the wrong side of each I square.

3. Place an I square on the 90-degree corner of H and stitch on the marked line as shown in Figure 7; trim seam to ¼" and press I to the right side to complete an H-I unit, again referring to Figure 7.

Figure 7

4. Repeat step 3 to complete a total of 34 H-I units.

5. To complete one Blue Diamond block, sew F to opposite sides of A, again referring to Figure 3, to make an A-F unit; press seams toward F.

6. Sew G to opposite long sides of the A-F unit, again referring to Figure 4, to make an A-F-G unit; press seams toward G.

7. Sew an H-I unit to opposite sides of the A-F-G unit to complete one block, again referring to Figure 5; press seams toward the H-I units.

8. Repeat steps 5–7 to complete a total of 17 Blue Diamond blocks.

Completing the Quilt

1. Join two Blue Diamond blocks and three Green Diamond blocks to make an X row as shown in Figure 8; press seams toward Blue Diamond blocks. Repeat to make four X rows.

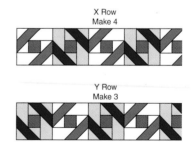

Figure 8

2. Join two Green Diamond blocks and three Blue Diamond blocks to make a Y row, again referring to Figure 8; press seams toward the Blue Diamond blocks. Repeat to make three Y rows.

Diamonds in Light & Dark
Placement Diagram 56" x 74"

3. Referring to the Placement Diagram, join the X and Y rows to complete the pieced center; press seams in one direction.

4. Join the J/K strips on the short ends to make one long strip; press seams open. Subcut strip into two 63½" J strips and two 47½" K strips.

5. Sew the J strips to opposite long sides and K strips to the top and bottom of the pieced center; press seams toward J and K strips.

6. Join one each M, N, O and P rectangles to make a pieced strip as shown in Figure 9; press seams in one direction. Repeat to make eight pieced strips.

Figure 9

7. Join the L strips on the short ends to make one long strip; press seams open. Subcut strip into two 45½" L strips.

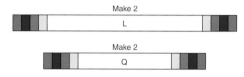

Figure 10

8. Sew the M end of a pieced strip to each end of each L and Q strip to make border strips as shown in Figure 10; press seams away from the L and Q strips.

9. Sew the pieced L strip to opposite long sides of the pieced center; press seams toward J strips.

10. Sew an R square to each end of each pieced Q strip; press seams toward R. Sew these strips to the top and bottom of the pieced center to complete the pieced top; press seams toward K strips.

11. Layer, quilt and bind referring to Finishing Your Quilt on page 80. ♦

Well-Connected Stars

DESIGN BY JUDITH SANDSTROM

The stars in this quilt are interconnected by colors.

Project Specifications

Skill Level: Advanced
Quilt Size: 66" x 84"
Block Size: 12" x 12"
Number of Blocks: 28

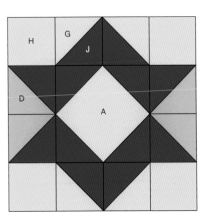

Yellow/Orange
12" x 12" Block
Make 4

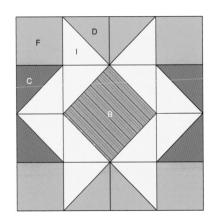

Yellow/Blue
12" x 12" Block
Make 8

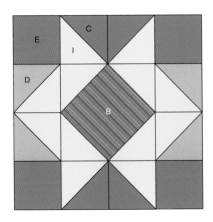

Blue/Yellow
12" x 12" Block
Make 8

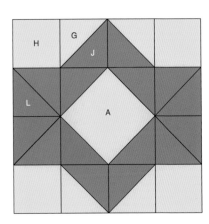

Yellow/Purple
12" x 12" Block
Make 4

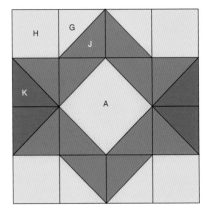

Yellow/Green
12" x 12" Block
Make 4

Materials

- ¼ yard each 4 blue stripes
- ⅓ yard green tonal
- ⅓ yard purple tonal
- ⅓ yard each 4 blue prints
- ½ yard each 4 yellow prints
- ⅔ yard cream/multicolored stripe
- 1¼ yards blue tonal
- 1⅜ yards orange print
- 1½ yards yellow tonal
- Batting 72" x 90"
- Backing 72" x 90"
- Neutral-color all-purpose thread
- Quilting thread
- Basic sewing tools and supplies

Cutting

1. Cut three 4¾" by fabric width strips yellow tonal; subcut strips into 24 (4¾") A squares.

2. Cut five 3⅞" by fabric width strips yellow tonal; subcut strips into 42 (3⅞") squares. Cut each square in half on one diagonal to make 84 G triangles.

3. Cut four 3½" by fabric width strips yellow tonal; subcut strips into 48 (3½") H squares.

4. Cut one 4¾" by fabric width strip each blue stripes; subcut strips into 25 (4¾") B squares.

5. Cut seven 3⅞" by fabric width strips blue tonal; subcut strips into 68 (3⅞") squares. Cut each square in half on one diagonal to make 136 C triangles.

6. Cut three 3½" by fabric width strips blue tonal; subcut strips into 32 (3½") E squares.

7. Cut nine 3⅞" by fabric width strips orange print; subcut strips into 88 (3⅞") squares. Cut each square in half on one diagonal to make 176 D triangles.

8. Cut three 3½" by fabric width strips orange print; subcut strips into 32 (3½") F squares.

9. Cut three 3⅞" by fabric width strips each yellow print; subcut strips into 24 (3⅞") squares each fabric. Cut each square in half on one diagonal to make 48 I triangles each fabric.

10. Cut two 3⅞" by fabric width strips each blue print; subcut strips into 18 (3⅞") squares each fabric. Cut each square in half on one diagonal to make 36 J triangles each fabric.

11. Cut two 3⅞" by fabric width strips green tonal; subcut strips into 20 (3⅞") squares. Cut each square in half on one diagonal to make 40 K triangles.

12. Cut two 3⅞" by fabric width strips purple tonal; subcut strips into 20 (3⅞") squares. Cut each square in half on one diagonal to make 40 L triangles.

13. Cut eight 2¼" by fabric width strips cream/multicolored stripe for binding.

Completing the Blue/Yellow Blocks

1. To make one Blue/Yellow block, select 12 matching I triangles, four each C and D triangles, four E squares and one B square.

2. Referring to block drawing, sew diagonal side of an I triangle to each side of B; press seams toward I.

3. Sew I to D along the diagonal to make a D-I unit as shown in Figure 1; press seam toward D. Repeat to make four D-I units. Repeat to make four C-I units, again referring to Figure 1.

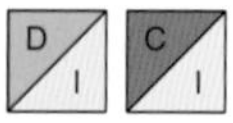

Figure 1

4. Join two D-I units to make a side unit as shown in Figure 2; press seam in one direction. Repeat to make two side units.

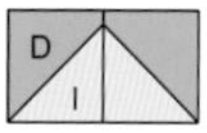

Figure 2

5. Sew a side unit to opposite sides of the B-I unit to complete the center row; press seams toward the B-I unit.

6. Join two C-I units and add E as shown in Figure 3 to make the top unit; press seams toward E. Repeat to make the bottom unit.

Figure 3

7. Sew the top and bottom units to the center row to complete one Blue/Yellow block as shown in Figure 4; press seams toward the center row.

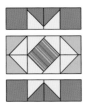

Figure 4

8. Repeat steps 1–7 to complete eight Blue/Yellow blocks.

Completing the Yellow/Blue Blocks

1. Using 12 matching I triangles, four each C and D triangles, four F squares and one B square for each block, complete eight Yellow/Blue blocks referring to Figure 5 and steps 2–7 of Completing the Blue/Yellow Blocks.

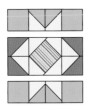

Figure 5

Completing the Yellow/Orange Blocks

1. Using 12 matching J triangles, four each D and G triangles, four H squares and one A square for each block, complete four Yellow/Orange blocks referring to Figure 6 and steps 2–7 of Completing the Blue/Yellow Blocks.

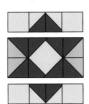

Figure 6

Completing the Yellow/Green Blocks

1. Using 12 matching J triangles, four each G and K triangles, four H squares and one A square for each block, complete four Yellow/Green blocks referring to Figure 7 and steps 2–7 of Completing the Blue/Yellow Blocks.

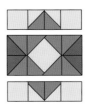

Figure 7

Completing the Yellow/Purple Blocks

1. Using 12 matching J triangles, four each G and L triangles, four H squares and one A square for each block, complete four Yellow/Purple blocks referring to Figure 8 and steps 2–7 of Completing the Blue/Yellow Blocks.

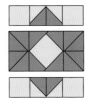

Figure 8

Completing the Sashing Units

1. Sew diagonal side of a C triangle to each side of A; press seams toward C.

2. Sew C to D along the diagonal to make a C-D unit as shown in Figure 9; press seam toward D. Repeat to make four C-D units.

3. Join two C-D units to make a top unit, again referring to Figure 9; press seam in one direction. Repeat to make two top units.

Figure 9

4. Sew a top unit to the top and bottom of the A-C unit to complete one blue/orange sashing unit as shown in Figure 10. Repeat to make six blue/orange sashing units.

Blue/orange
Make 6

Figure 10

5. Repeat steps 1–4 with A, C and D pieces as shown in Figure 11 to complete six orange/blue sashing units.

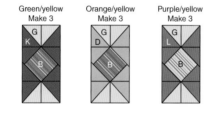

| Orange/blue | Green/yellow | Orange/yellow | Purple/yellow |
| Make 6 | Make 3 | Make 3 | Make 3 |

Figure 11

6. Repeat steps 1–4 with B, K and G pieces to complete three green/yellow sashing units, again referring to Figure 11.

7. Repeat steps 1–4 with B, D and G pieces to complete three orange/yellow sashing units, again referring to Figure 11.

8. Repeat steps 1–4 with B, L and G to complete three purple/yellow sashing units, again referring to Figure 11.

Completing the Top

1. Join four Blue/Yellow blocks with three orange/blue sashing units to complete a yellow/orange row referring to Figure 12; repeat to make two yellow/orange rows. Press seams toward sashing units.

2. Join four Yellow/Green blocks with three green/yellow sashing units to complete one green row, again referring to Figure 12; press seams toward the blocks.

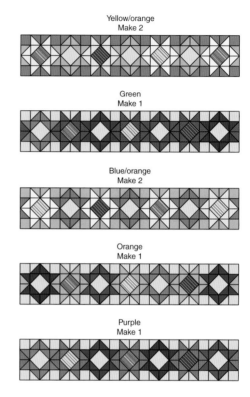

Yellow/orange
Make 2

Green
Make 1

Blue/orange
Make 2

Orange
Make 1

Purple
Make 1

Figure 12

3. Join four Yellow/Blue blocks with three blue/orange sashing units to complete one blue/orange row, again referring to Figure 12; repeat to make two blue/orange rows. Press seams toward sashing units.

4. Join four Yellow/Orange blocks with three orange/yellow sashing units to complete one orange row, again referring to Figure 12; press seams toward blocks.

5. Join four Yellow/Purple blocks with three purple/yellow sashing units to complete one purple row, again referring to Figure 12; press seams toward blocks.

6. Arrange and join the rows referring to the Placement Diagram for positioning; press seams in one direction.

7. Layer, quilt and bind referring to Finishing Your Quilt on page 80. ♦

Well-Connected Stars
Placement Diagram 66" x 84"

Polka-Dot Party

DESIGN BY CONNIE KAUFFMAN

Bright polka dots make this throw a cheerful addition to any room.

Crossed Dots
6" x 6" Block
Make 12

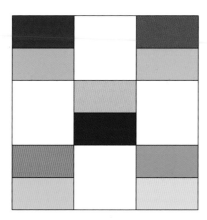

Dot Nine-Patch
6" x 6" Block
Make 13

Project Specifications

Skill Level: Beginner
Quilt Size: 42" x 42"
Block Size: 6" x 6"
Number of Blocks: 25

Materials

- 1 fat quarter each 6 or more polka-dot fabrics
- 1 fat quarter each 5 bright fabrics
- ⅜ yard white tonal
- ½ yard white background with dots (white dot)
- ½ yard green background with dots (green dot)
- 1 yard purple background with dots (purple dot)
- Backing 48" x 48"
- Batting 48" x 48"
- Neutral-color all-purpose thread
- Quilting thread
- Basic sewing tools and supplies

Cutting

1. Cut four 2½" by fabric width strips white tonal; subcut strips into 52 (2½") A squares.

2. Cut 65 (1½" x 2½") B rectangles from polka-dot fat quarters. Repeat to cut 65 B rectangles from bright fat quarters.

3. Cut six 7¼" squares each purple dot and white dot; cut each square in half on both diagonals to make 24 each C purple dot triangles and D white dot triangles.

4. Cut two 3½" x 30½" E strips and two 3½" x 36½" F strips green dot.

5. Cut approximately 40 (2" x 7" to 2" x 11") border strips from polka-dot and bright fat quarters.

6. Cut five 2¼" by fabric width strips purple dot for binding.

Piecing the Dot Nine-Patch Blocks

1. Join one each polka-dot and bright B rectangles on the 2½" sides to make a B unit; repeat for 65 B units.

2. To complete one Dot Nine-Patch block, join two B units with A to make a row as shown in Figure 1; repeat for two rows. Press seams toward B units.

Make 2

Make 1

Figure 1

3. Join one B unit with two A squares to make a row, again referring to Figure 1; press seams toward B unit.

4. Join the rows to complete one Dot Nine-Patch block as shown in Figure 2; press seams in one direction. Repeat for 13 blocks.

Figure 2

Piecing the Crossed Dots Blocks

1. To piece one Crossed Dots block, sew C to D as shown in Figure 3; repeat for two C-D units. Press seams toward C.

Figure 3

2. Join two C-D units to complete one Crossed Dots block as shown in Figure 4; press seams in one direction. Repeat for 12 blocks.

Figure 4

Completing the Quilt

1. Join three Dot Nine-Patch blocks with two Crossed Dots blocks to make a row referring to Figure 5; press seams toward Crossed Dots blocks. Repeat for three rows.

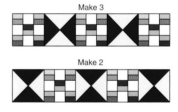

Make 3

Make 2

Figure 5

2. Join three Crossed Dots blocks with two Dot Nine-Patch blocks to make a row, again referring to Figure 5; press seams toward Crossed Dots blocks. Repeat for two rows.

3. Join the rows referring to the Placement Diagram; press seams in one direction.

4. Sew E strips to opposite sides and F strips to the top and bottom of the pieced center; press seams toward strips.

5. Join the border strips on short ends to make one long strip, alternating polka-dot and bright strips; press seams in one direction.

6. Cut two strips each 36½" G and 42½" I, and four strips 39½" H.

7. Sew G to opposite sides and H to the top and bottom of the pieced center; press seams toward E and F. Sew

H to opposite sides and I to the top and bottom of the pieced center; press seams toward H and I.

8. Layer, quilt and bind referring to Finishing Your Quilt on page 80. ♦

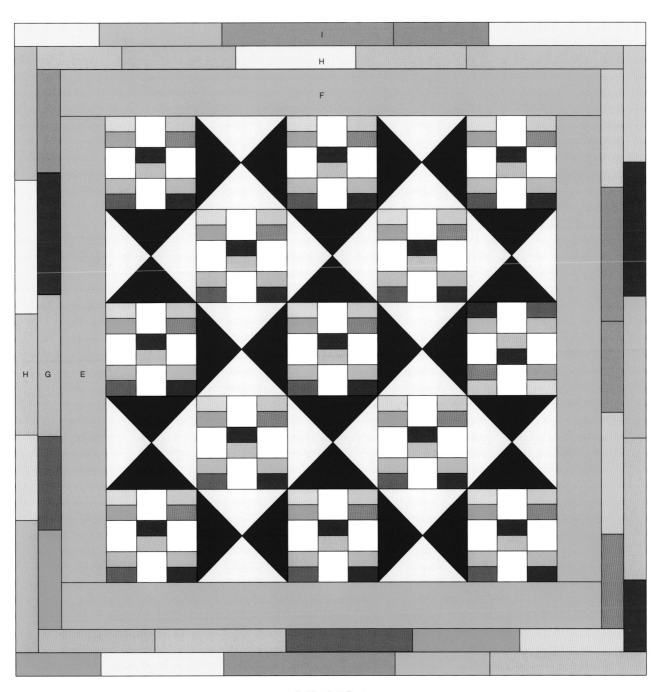

Polka-Dot Party
Placement Diagram 42" x 42"

String Stars

DESIGN BY SUE HARVEY

The star points for each star are unique, making this an excellent quilt for using scraps of all sizes.

PROJECT SPECIFICATIONS

Skill Level: Advanced
Quilt Size: 75" x 87½"

MATERIALS

- Scraps to total 5 yards
- ¾ yard blue print
- 2¾ yards pink print
- 4 yards muslin
- Backing 81" x 94"
- Batting 81" x 94"
- All-purpose thread to match fabrics
- Quilting thread
- Template material
- Basic sewing tools and supplies

Cutting

1. Prepare templates for A and B/C using patterns given. cut A as directed on pattern.

2. Referring to Figure 1, place the B/C template on one fold of template material to make the C template. Place the long edge of C on one fold of template material to make the B template, again referring to Figure 1.

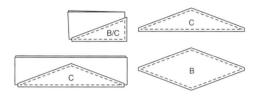

Figure 1

3. Cut A from muslin as directed on template patterns.

4. Cut B and C from the pink print as directed on template patterns.

5. Cut nine 2¼" by fabric width strips blue print for binding.

String-Piecing the Star Points

1. Cut 20–30 scrap strips in widths from 1½"–5", varying in width from one end of the strip to the other end as shown in Figure 2. **Note:** *Cut additional strips as needed while piecing the points.*

Figure 2

2. Place a strip right side up on the wide end of a muslin A piece as shown in Figure 3; pin in place.

Figure 3

3. Place a second strip right sides together with the first strip with raw edges aligned as shown in Figure 4; stitch ¼" from the aligned edges through all layers, again referring to Figure 4. Press the second strip to the right side, again referring to Figure 4.

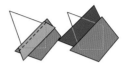

Figure 4

4. Repeat step 3 with additional strips to cover the A piece to complete one star point as shown in Figure 5; trim strips even with muslin A, again referring to Figure 5. **Note:** *Three or four strips were used to cover each star point.*

Figure 5

5. Repeat steps 2–4 to complete 168 star points.

Completing the Quilt

1. Join four star points to complete a star unit as shown in Figure 6; press seams in opposite directions and to one side. Repeat to complete 42 star units.

Figure 6

2. Join six star units with five B pieces and two C pieces to make a row as shown in Figure 7, setting the B pieces into the adjacent star units and the C pieces into each end; press seams toward B and C. Repeat to complete seven rows.

Figure 7

3. Join the rows with six B pieces referring to the Placement Diagram; press seams toward B.

4. Set a C piece into each star unit in the top and bottom row to complete the top; press seams toward C.

5. Layer, quilt and bind referring to Finishing Your Quilt on page 80. ♦

String Stars
Placement Diagram 75" x 87¹/₂"

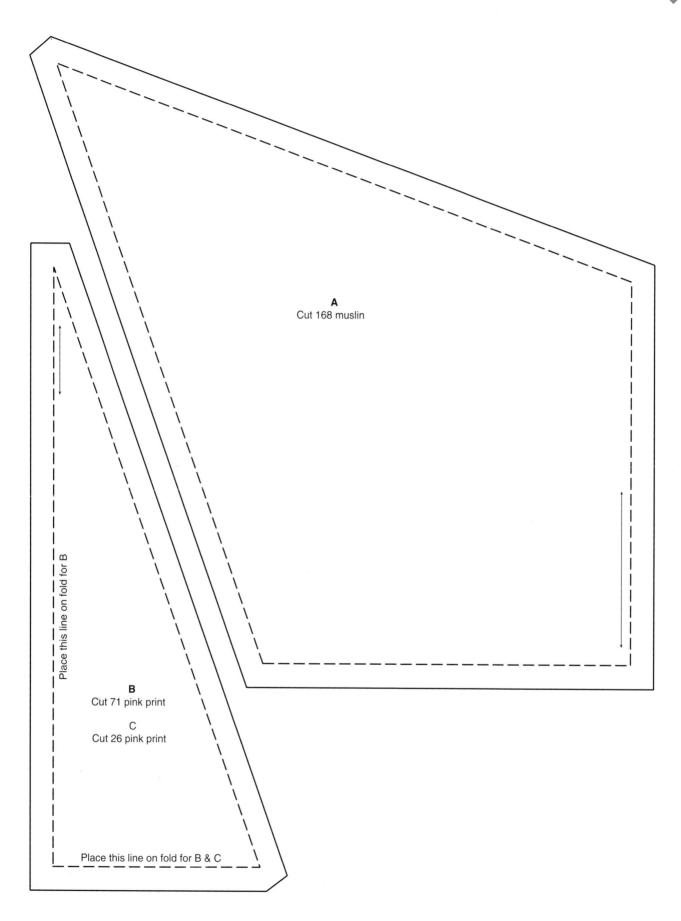

A
Cut 168 muslin

Place this line on fold for B

B
Cut 71 pink print

C
Cut 26 pink print

Place this line on fold for B & C

Quilt-Making Basics

Materials & Supplies

Fabrics

One hundred percent cotton fabrics are recommended for making quilts. Fabrics may be prewashed, depending on your preference but, be sure to do the same thing to all fabrics in the project. Whether you prewash or not, be sure your fabrics are colorfast and won't run onto each other when washed after use.

Fabrics are woven with threads going in a crosswise and lengthwise direction. The threads cross at right angles—the more threads per inch, the stronger the fabric.

The crosswise threads will stretch a little. The lengthwise threads will not stretch at all. Cutting the fabric at a 45-degree angle to the crosswise and lengthwise threads produces a bias edge which stretches a great deal when pulled as shown in Figure 1.

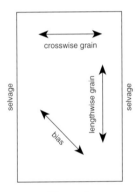

Figure 1

For the patterns in this book that contain templates, pay careful attention careful attention to the grain lines marked with arrows. These arrows indicate that the piece should be placed on the lengthwise grain with the arrow running on one thread as shown in Figure 2.

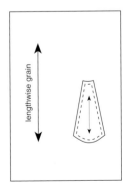

Figure 2

Thread

For most piecing, good-quality cotton or cotton-covered polyester is the thread of choice. Inexpensive polyester threads are not recommended because they can cut the fibers of cotton fabrics.

Choose a color thread that will match or blend with the fabrics in your quilt. For projects pieced with dark- and light-colored fabrics choose a neutral thread color, such as a medium gray, as a compromise between colors. Test by stitching a sample seam.

Batting

Batting is the material used to give a quilt loft or thickness. It also adds warmth.

Some qualities to look for in batting are drapability, resistance to fiber migration, loft and softness.

Tools & Equipment

There are few truly essential tools and little equipment required for quilt making. Basics include needles (hand-sewing and quilting betweens), pins (long, thin, sharp pins are best), sharp scissors or shears, a thimble, template materials (plastic or cardboard), marking tools (chalk marker, water-erasable pen and a No. 2 pencil are a few) and a quilting frame or hoop. For piecing and/or quilting by machine, add a sewing machine to the list.

Other sewing basics such as a seam ripper, pincushion, measuring tape and an iron are also necessary. For making strip-pieced quilts, a rotary cutter, mat and speciality rulers are often used.

Construction Methods

Traditional Templates

There are two types of templates—those that include a ¼" seam allowance and those that don't.

Choose the template material and the pattern. Transfer the pattern shapes to the template material with a sharp No. 2 lead pencil. Write the pattern name, piece letter or number, grain line and number to cut for one block or whole quilt on each piece as shown in Figure 3.

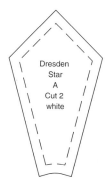

Figure 3

Some patterns require a reversed piece as shown in Figure 4. These patterns are labeled with an R after the piece letter; for example, B and BR. To reverse a template, first cut the fabric with the labeled side up and then with the labeled side down. Or, place two layers of fabric with right sides together and cut two pieces at once; one will be reversed.

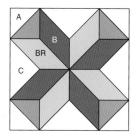

Figure 4

Machine-Piecing

If making templates, include the ¼" seam allowance on the template for machine-piecing. Place template on the wrong side of the fabric and butt pieces together when tracing.

Set machine on 2.5 or 12–15 stitches per inch. Join pieces, beginning and ending sewing at the end of the fabric patch. No backstitching is necessary when machine-stitching.

Quick-Cutting

Templates can be completely eliminated when using a rotary cutter with a plastic ruler and mat to cut fabric strips.

When rotary-cutting strips, straighten raw edges of fabric by folding fabric in half or in fourths across the width as shown in Figure 5. Press down flat; place ruler on fabric square with edge of fabric and make one cut from the folded edge to the outside edge. If strips are not straightened, a wavy strip will result as shown in Figure 6.

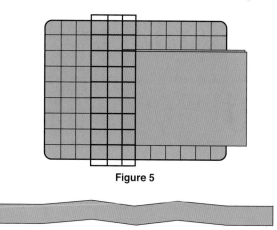

Figure 5

Figure 6

Always cut away from your body, holding the ruler firmly with the non-cutting hand.

Quick-Piecing Method

Lay pieces to be joined under the presser foot of the sewing machine right sides together. Sew an exact ¼" seam allowance to the end of the piece; place another unit right next to the first one and continue sewing, adding a piece after every stitched piece, until all of the pieces are used up as shown in Figure 7.

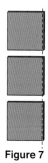

Figure 7

When sewing is finished, cut the threads that join the pieces apart. Press seam toward the darker fabric.

Finishing Your Quilt

Step 1. Sandwich the batting between the completed top and prepared backing; pin or baste layers together to hold. **Note:** *If using basting spray to hold layers together, refer to instructions on the product container for use.*

Step 2. Quilt as desired by hand or machine; remove pins or basting. Trim excess backing and batting even with quilt top.

Step 3. Join binding strips on short ends to make one long strip. Fold the strip in half along length with wrong sides together; press.

Step 4. Sew binding to quilt edges, mitering corners and overlapping ends. Fold binding to the back side and stitch in place to finish.

Metric Conversion Charts

Metric Conversions

Canada/U.S. Measurement		Multiplied by		Metric Measurement
yards	x	.9144	=	metres (m)
yards	x	91.44	=	centimetres (cm)
inches	x	2.54	=	centimetres (cm)
inches	x	25.40	=	millimetres (mm)
inches	x	.0254	=	metres (m)

Canada/U.S. Measurement		Multiplied by		Metric Measurement
centimetres	x	.3937	=	inches
metres	x	1.0936	=	yards

Standard Equivalents

Canada/U.S. Measurement		Metric Measurement		
⅛ inch	=	3.20 mm	=	0.32 cm
¼ inch	=	6.35 mm	=	0.635 cm
⅜ inch	=	9.50 mm	=	0.95 cm
½ inch	=	12.70 mm	=	1.27 cm
⅝ inch	=	15.90 mm	=	1.59 cm
¾ inch	=	19.10 mm	=	1.91 cm
⅞ inch	=	22.20 mm	=	2.22 cm
1 inch	=	25.40 mm	=	2.54 cm
⅛ yard	=	11.43 cm	=	0.11 m
¼ yard	=	22.86 cm	=	0.23 m
⅜ yard	=	34.29 cm	=	0.34 m
½ yard	=	45.72 cm	=	0.46 m
⅝ yard	=	57.15 cm	=	0.57 m
¾ yard	=	68.58 cm	=	0.69 m
⅞ yard	=	80.00 cm	=	0.80 m
1 yard	=	91.44 cm	=	0.91 m
1⅛ yards	=	102.87 cm	=	1.03 m
1¼ yards	=	114.30 cm	=	1.14 m

Canada/U.S. Measurement		Metric Measurement		
1⅜ yards	=	125.73 cm	=	1.26 m
1½ yards	=	137.16 cm	=	1.37 m
1⅝ yards	=	148.59 cm	=	1.49 m
1¾ yards	=	160.02 cm	=	1.60 m
1⅞ yards	=	171.44 cm	=	1.71 m
2 yards	=	182.88 cm	=	1.83 m
2⅛ yards	=	194.31 cm	=	1.94 m
2¼ yards	=	205.74 cm	=	2.06 m
2⅜ yards	=	217.17 cm	=	2.17 m
2½ yards	=	228.60 cm	=	2.29 m
2⅝ yards	=	240.03 cm	=	2.40 m
2¾ yards	=	251.46 cm	=	2.51 m
2⅞ yards	=	262.88 cm	=	2.63 m
3 yards	=	274.32 cm	=	2.74 m
3⅛ yards	=	285.75 cm	=	2.86 m
3¼ yards	=	297.18 cm	=	2.97 m
3⅜ yards	=	308.61 cm	=	3.09 m
3½ yards	=	320.04 cm	=	3.20 m
3⅝ yards	=	331.47 cm	=	3.31 m
3¾ yards	=	342.90 cm	=	3.43 m
3⅞ yards	=	354.32 cm	=	3.54 m
4 yards	=	365.76 cm	=	3.66 m
4⅛ yards	=	377.19 cm	=	3.77 m
4¼ yards	=	388.62 cm	=	3.89 m
4⅜ yards	=	400.05 cm	=	4.00 m
4½ yards	=	411.48 cm	=	4.11 m
4⅝ yards	=	422.91 cm	=	4.23 m
4¾ yards	=	434.34 cm	=	4.34 m
4⅞ yards	=	445.76 cm	=	4.46 m
5 yards	=	457.20 cm	=	4.57 m